WOMEN UNDER APARTHEID

This book shows how African women under apartheid are ~~oppressed as black~~ people, as workers and as women. It shows too their part in the struggle for freedom.

Through the apartheid system the wealth and resources of South Africa are controlled by the ruling white minority.

The 80% of the population who are black are denied political rights. Amongst the black majority, the Africans, who are 70% of the population of South Africa, are the most oppressed.

The Whites have taken most of the land (87% of it). Most Africans must find work in the areas declared "White" since that is where most of the economic activity of South Africa takes place. If they are not given a job there, they must remain in the bantustans, the small part of the country (13%) that is allocated by the Whites to Africans, where there is little work and great poverty. Even more women (6.1m) than men (5.2m) are confined to the bantustans.

Many of those who work in the "White" areas are contract labourers, only allowed to stay for a limited period of one year at a time. African workers have only minimal rights to organise in trade unions in order to try to increase the very low wages they are generally paid. As a group African women are paid the lowest wages of all, if they can find work.

In these ways a predominantly migrant labour system is maintained, with plentiful reserves of cheap labour.

This is part of what women are seeking to change by participating in the liberation struggle.

WOMEN UNDER APARTHEID

In photographs and text

International Defence and Aid Fund for Southern Africa, in co-operation with the United Nations Centre Against Apartheid
London, 1981.

The International Defence and Aid Fund for Southern Africa is a humanitarian organisation which has worked consistently for peaceful and constructive solutions to the problems created by racial oppression in Southern Africa.

It sprang from Christian and humanist opposition to the evils and injustices of apartheid in South Africa. It is dedicated to the achievement of free, democratic, non-racial societies throughout Southern Africa.

The objects of the Fund are:–

  (i)   to aid, defend and rehabilitate the victims of unjust legislation and oppressive and arbitrary procedures,

 (ii)   to support their families and dependents,

(iii)   to keep the conscience of the world alive to the issues at stake.

In accordance with these three objects, the Fund distributes its humanitarian aid to the victims of racial injustice without any discrimination on grounds of race, colour, religious or political affiliation. The only criterion is that of genuine need.

For many years, under clause (iii) of its objects, the Fund has run a comprehensive information service on affairs in Southern Africa. This includes visual documentation. It produces a regular news bulletin 'FOCUS' on Political Repression in Southern Africa, and publishes pamphlets and books on all aspects of life in Southern Africa.

The Fund prides itself on the strict accuracy of all its information.

This book was prepared by IDAF Research, Information and Publicity Department. It is derived from a photographic exhibition prepared by IDAF at the request of the United Nations.

ISBN No. 0 904759 45 8

CONTENTS

INTRODUCTION:
The Migrant Labour System

"That is in fact the entire basis of our policy as far as the white economy is concerned, namely a system of migratory labour."
> — G. F. van L. Froneman, Deputy Minister of Justice, Mines and Planning, House of Assembly, 6 February 1968.[1]

"There must be no illusions about this, because if our policy is taken to its full logical conclusion as far as the Black people are concerned, there will not be one Black man with South African citizenship."
> — Dr. Connie Mulder, Minister of Plural Relations and Development, House of Assembly, 7 February 1978.[2]

The fundamental condition affecting the lives of African women in South Africa is the migrant labour system, which keeps apartheid's labour cheap—and chained.

The labour structure of South Africa has developed on the basis of migratory labour. African men who come into the "white" towns to work, generally have to leave their wives and families in the reserves.

This depresses the wages paid to the men because in theory their families are able to live on the proceeds of subsistence agriculture at "home". It also prevents Africans from becoming integrated into the "white" urban economy, and demanding services, and rights.

However the history of South Africa has also been one of industrialisation, with a consequent movement of African families to the growing cities.

In the face of this movement the migrant labour system has been maintained by increasingly harsh legislation and administrative procedures: the tightening of the Pass Laws, which regulate the movement of Africans; the resettlement of what a Government Minister called "superfluous appendages" (women, children and the aged and infirm) in the reserves or "homelands", or "bantustans" as they have become known.

Now bantustans—such as the Transkei, BophuthaTswana, Venda and Ciskei—are being given a spurious independence.

African family in the Transkei Bantustan.   Photo: Tony McGrath

This enables the South African government to treat all their "nationals" as *foreigners with no rights at all* in "white" South Africa—that is, in 87% of the country, which is ruled by and for the whites who form 17% of the population.

Large numbers of bantustan "nationals" may be "endorsed out" (deported) to a "country" they have never seen. One effect of these measures has been to aggravate the overcrowding and poverty of the bantustans.

Women have increasingly been forced off the land and drawn into the migrant labour system, moving to the cities to work. There they, like the men, are accommodated either in single quarters belonging to their employers, or in single-sex "bachelor hostels" whether they are married or not. In these hostels, no members of the opposite sex may be entertained in rooms, and no children are allowed.

House in Soweto, Johannesburg. Photo: Abisag Tüllmann

African mother and children Cape Town area.   Photo: Steve Bloom

These are the prospects offered by apartheid to millions of African women: either single accommodation in the cities, without their children; or the desolation of the bantustans, deprived of their families and without amenities—and in which they will in any case spend their childhood and old age. Any family life will be fleeting; husbands, and perhaps children, hardly known to them.

As migrants, African women work largely as domestic servants for white women. The South African author Hilda Bernstein observes that after childbirth "the primary role of a white woman becomes that of consumer and a living display, through leisure and adornment, of her husband's wealth."[3] Some white women are prepared to transcend this role. For instance, members of the Black Sash (photo opposite) demonstrate against apartheid and try to help victims of the pass laws. Some white women have been imprisoned or detained, or have left South Africa as exiles. However, they are few in number.

[1] *House of Assembly Debates,* 6/2/68.
[2] *House of Assembly Debates,* 7/2/78.
[3] Hilda Bernstein, *For their Triumphs and for their Tears* (IDAF London, 1978) p.61.

White family, with black servant, in Johannesburg.   Photo: Tony McGrath

PROVINCIAL
BUILDING
SOCIETY
Regverdigheid
eis 'n
NASIONALE
KONVENSIE
van
ALLE
RASSE
Justice
demands
a
NATIONAL
CONVENTION
of
ALL
RACES

1. FAMILY LIFE

"We are giving them the choice: they must send their children back to the home-lands themselves . . . The law states that they are illegally in the area, so they have to go. It's as simple as that."
— Mr. Coen Kotze, Bantu Affairs Department, Alexandra Township, Johannesburg, 1972.[1]

African mother and children in Johannesburg area.

Photo: Eli Weinberg

Interior of Soweto house. Photo: John Seymour

Family life is devastated by apartheid, and in particular by the migrant system. The South African sociologist Dr. Trudi Thomas describes what happens when men leave their families in the bantustans to work in the cities:

"Broken marriages and desertion and faithlessness are distressingly common, and the reason is clear . . . African relationships, as in all cultures, depend on loyalty and affection. These bonds in turn depend upon mutual support and comfort, on shared experiences and responsibilities, and companionships. All these must be sacrificed when the man goes away for long periods . . ."[2]

Even where a husband and wife are working in the same city, they may be prevented from living together. One of them may live on the premises where they are employed, as in the case of many women who work as domestic servants; or in quarters such as a "bachelor hostel" where no spouses or children are allowed. The first option may also mean separation from husband and children.

African grandmother and children in Johannesburg area. Photo: UN/Contact (over page)

There may be grievous consequences for children born into these circumstances. For unless somebody in the bantustans can be found to look after these children and provide for them there may be literally nowhere for them to go. For an unmarried woman to have a baby may thus be a calamity; but as stable relationships are prevented or destroyed by the system, births to unmarried women are becoming the rule. In Durban in the 1970s, between 59 and 64 of every 100 African babies were born to unmarried women; in East London, between 50 and 68.[3]

Numbers of African children are being abandoned altogether. The Johannesburg Child Welfare Society stated in 1978 that the number of such cases had increased from 2,618 in 1976 to over 4,000 in 1977.[4]

Dr. Thomas writes: "These are the children of resentment, and deprivation. Deprived of affection and sufficient food . . . Denied self-respect. Nobody comforts them, nobody cares. Unprotected, unstimulated, untutored, unoccupied, left to their own devices."[5]

However, despite these enormous problems, the human spirit asserts itself and families somehow manage to survive.

AFRICAN POPULATION IN SOUTH AFRICA IN 1980

	"White Urban Areas"	"White Rural Areas"	Bantustans	Total
Total	5.3m (25.3%)	4.3m (20.6%)	11.3m (54%)	21.0m (100%)
Men	3.0m (28.5%)	2.3m (21.8%)	5.2m (49.6%)	10.5m (100%)
Women	2.3m (22.2%)	2.0m (19.4%)	6.1m (58.4%)	10.5m (100%)
No. of men for every 100 women	129	113	85	100

Source: C. E. W. Simkins *"The distribution of the African population of South Africa by Age, Sex and Region-type, 1960, 1970, 1980"*. Saldru Working Paper No. 32, South African Labour and Development Research Unit January 1981.

---

[1] Hilda Bernstein, *For their Triumphs and for their Tears*, (IDAF, London, 1978) p. 31.
[2] Trudi Thomas, "The seeds of deprivation", *Black Sash*, May 1974; quoted in Hilda Bernstein, *For their Triumphs and for their Tears*, p. 30.
[3] Hilda Bernstein, op. cit. p. 29.
[4] South African Institute of Race Relations, *Survey* 1978, p. 484.
[5] Hilda Bernstein, op. cit., p. 29.

African mother and coloured father with family in Cape Town. An illegal marriage as parents should live in respective group areas.

Photo: John Seymour

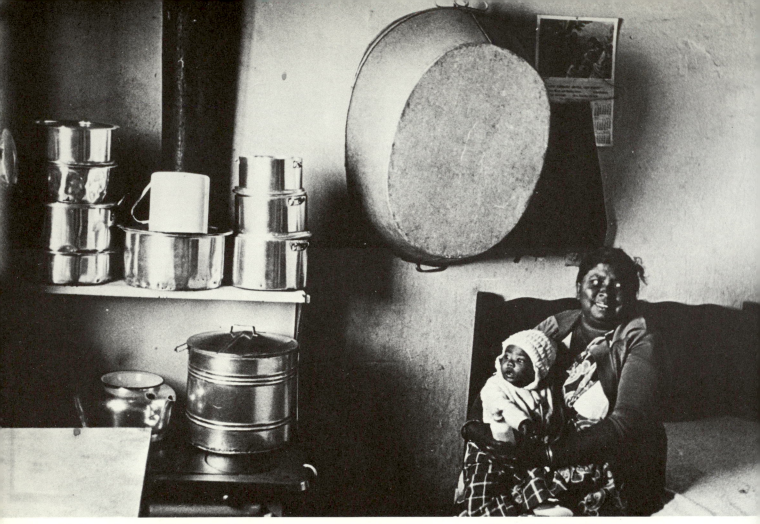

Indian mother and child, Lenasia, Johannesburg.

Photo: Rick Kollektiff

African family, Cape Town area.

Coloured family in Newclare township,
Johannesburg.   Photo: John Seymour
(opposite page)

Coloured family, Cape Town area.
 Photo: Tony McGrath

Family evicted and removed
under Group Areas Act.
Photo: Jurgen Schadeberg

2. RESETTLEMENT

"But those Bantu in our white areas who are not economically active . . . should be channelled back to their own homelands . . . Approximately 900,000 Bantu have been settled elsewhere under the Nationalist Party regime over the past few years, since 1959. Surely this is no mean achievement; on the contrary, it is a tremendous achievement."

— Dr. P. J. Koornhof, Deputy Minister of Bantu Administration and Development, House of Assembly, 1969.[1]

Old woman with possessions outside her home which is being demolished.   Photographer Unknown

Africans are not only being moved from "white" areas to the bantustans but, under "consolidation" procedures, by which tribal groups are separated, they are moved within the bantustans as well.

The number of Africans forcibly removed or "re-located" is enormous. Complete information is difficult to obtain, but at least three million have been affected since 1948, without taking into account people who have been moved within the bantustans.[2] Some estimates are much higher.

It is primarily women who are affected by the removals. Either in their "traditional" role as subsistence farmers in the bantustans, or as a result of their especially disadvantaged status in the cities, women form the majority of those removed.

The rights of Africans to reside in urban areas have been dependent on conditions defined in Section 10 of the Urban Areas Act. The basic qualifications for such rights are that a person must *either* have been born in an area and lived continuously there since; *or* must have worked continuously in the area for 10 years for one employer or lived continuously there for 15 years with official permission. Under Section 10(1)c of the Act, wives and dependent children of men qualified in either of these ways are also qualified, provided they are ordinarily resident with them.

It has been made difficult for women to obtain even these restricted rights. In 1964 the Bantu Laws Amendment Act placed a total ban on the further entry of women into the urban areas, other than on a visitor's permit. The following year a court ruled that all African women living in the urban areas on 24 June 1952 should have registered within *72 hours of that date* to qualify for any residential rights. Their period of residence was to be reckoned from the date of registration and not from the date on which they actually commenced living in the area.

Waiting for train to resettlement camp. Photographer Unknown

(opposite)
KwaZulu "Homeland".
Photo: Stan Winer

Most women were thus disqualified and many were deported to the bantustans.[3]

In other ways, too, women are disadvantaged by the residential laws:

★ "continuous" periods of residence are more difficult for them to fulfil, because many women go to parents in country areas for the birth of their babies;

★ women are prohibited from being registered tenants in the townships, so that they become homeless if widowed, divorced, separated or deserted, thus facing eviction, and deportation to a bantustan;

The South African author Hilda Bernstein describes resettlement:

"The act of removal itself can be a bitter and terrible experience. From homes in towns where there were some amenities — schools, shops, transport, clinics; or from lands regarded as ancestral where the enlarged African family could thrive in all its warmth; to arid settlements in distant places they must go . . . deposited in Limehill, Welcome Valley, Mdantsane, Dimbaza, spewed off Government lorries with what possessions they are able to take . . . in countryside which is often grotesque and desolate, they will be taken to a few rows of unshaded iron or asbestos huts without floors or ceilings, or to tents . . . Bewilderment strikes to the very roots of the soul; apathy in the face of problems too great to overcome; sickness decimating those least able to resist; death . . . the burden is carried by the women."[4]

Not only Africans are removed. Under the Group Areas Act, more than half a million Indian and Coloured (mixed race) people have been resettled.[5]

[1] Hilda Bernstein, *For their Triumphs and for their Tears*, (IDAF, London, 1978) p. 15.
[2] Barbara Rogers, *Mass population removals in apartheid South Africa (1978-80)*, UN Centre Against Apartheid 27/80, 1980.
[3] David Davis, *African Workers and Apartheid* (IDAF, London, 1978) pp. 6-7.
[4] Hilda Bernstein, Ibid., p. 16.
[5] Hilda Bernstein, Ibid., p. 15.

Indian family, evicted under Group Areas Act, at resettlement camp.   Photographer Unknown

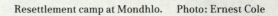
Resettlement camp at Mondhlo.   Photo: Ernest Cole

"Welcome Valley" resettlement camp, Illinge, Natal.   Photo: John Seymour

Weenen resettlement
camp, Natal.
Photo: John Seymour

Queueing for water brought to resettlement area in tanker.   Photographer Unknown

Morsgat resettlement camp, Western Transvaal.   Photographer Unknown

In Transkei Bantustan.
Photo: Tony McGrath

(opposite)

**Resettlement camp in
KwaZulu.**

Photo: Stan Winer

Resettlement camp at Mondhlo.

Photo: Ernest Cole

3. WOMEN AT WORK

"African women want employment. There are no conventions and traditional taboos that restrain them from working outside the home. Illiteracy and inadequate schooling are obstacles, but hardly more so for them than for the men ... the general level of education is much the same for both sexes. Underemployment among African women is a result of land hunger, insufficient utilization of human and natural resources, and discrimination against women on grounds of both sex and race."
— H. J. Simons, *African Women: their Legal Status in South Africa.*[1]

Road sweepers in Soweto.

Photo: Rick Kollektiff

The old apartheid pattern by which African women stayed in the reserves and did subsistence farming while the men went to work in the "white" cities has changed.

The overcrowding and escalating poverty of the bantustans[2] means that many women have been driven off the land. Under sexually discriminatory laws women have no rights to land in the bantustans and are often refused any land allocation by the government-appointed chiefs.[3]

Women are thus faced with the prospect of trying to find employment in the bantustans or joining the stream of migrant labourers to the cities.

Collecting wood.   Photo: Tony McGrath

FEMALE BANTU LABOUR BUREAU
BANTOE-ARBEIDSBURO (VROUENS)
LEKGOTLA LE MESEBETSI LA BASADI
INDAWO YEMISEBENZI YA ABAFAZI

Labour bureau for
women in Johannesburg.
Photo: Rick Kollektiff

When compared to the population of the bantustans—six million women live there and five million men[4]—work is almost non-existent.

The South African Government's own Corporation for Economic Development has admitted that the creation of jobs in and near the bantustans is completely inadequate for meeting the increase in unemployment inside the bantustans.[5]

Wages in the bantustans are very low. Several firms in Babelegi, Bophutatswana were reported to be paying many women workers rates between R7.50 and R10 a week (between £4.20 and £5.60, or $9.75 and $13.00 approximately) in 1980, at a time when the Poverty Datum Line was around R40 a week.[6]

The 1970 census showed that a quarter of all African women were employed, compared with a half of all African men.

Most African women who were employed worked either as domestic servants (38%) or as farm labourers (35%).[7]

Subsistence farming in the Transvaal.   Photo: August Sycholt

Sugar cane workers.
Photo: Tony McGrath

(previous page)   (opposite)
Farm workers in maize field.   Grape harvesting in Western Cape.
Photo: Tony McGrath   Photo: Tony McGrath

Nannies minding white
child.
Photo: Tony McGrath

Nanny minding white
children.
Photo: Tony McGrath

Servant exercising dog. Note nanny carrying white child on her back.　Photographer Unknown

(opposite)　Two servants carry sunshade and other beach equipment for white employer.　Photographer Unknown

Very few African women have managed to reach the professions, or even the white-collar level of work. In 1970 African female professional, administrative, clerical and sales workers all put together totalled only 4.4% of the total number of African women in employment.[8] Most of these were doing nursing or teaching, the only two professions that have traditionally been open to African women.

Nurses returning from work at Baragwanath hospital near Soweto.   Photo: Peter Magubane

Teacher.
Photo: Ernest Cole

In a shoe factory.
Photo: Tony McGrath

Even outside the bantustans, wages are desperately low, particularly in those areas where women are mainly employed.

The agricultural census on 1976 gave the national average wage of domestic employees on farms—one of the largest areas of employment for African women—as a total value, including rations, of R16.50 (approximately £8.00; US$16.00) per week.[9]

A 1979 survey of white households in the Eastern Cape revealed that domestic servants worked over 60 hours a week for an average wage of R23.00 per month.[10]

In industry things are not much better. In the laundry, cleaning and dyeing trade in 1978, the wage for an African woman was R18.50 per week.[11]

However the most important feature of employment for the majority of African women is the lack of it, outside the most menial forms of drudgery.

1 Hurst, London, 1968.
2 e.g. production of the two staple crops, maize and sorghum, fell 40% and 50% respectively in the decade 1958—1968. See Barbara Rogers, *Divide and Rule* (IDAF, London, 1980) p. 49.
3 Barbara Rogers, Ibid., p. 50.
4 C. Simkins, op. cit., p. 21.
5 Barbara Rogers, op. cit., p. 112.
6 *Post* 26.8.80; *Sunday Post* 14.9.80; South African Institute of Race Relations, *Survey* 1980, p. 84.
7 Hilda Bernstein, op. cit., pp. 36-7, pp. 69-70.
8 Hilda Bernstein, Ibid., p. 69.
9 Ibid., p. 207.
10 Jacklyn Cock, *Maids and Madams: a study in the politics of exploitation,* Raven Press, Johannesburg, 1980, quoted in *South African Outlook,* November 1979, pp. 165-6.
11 South African Institute of Race Relations, *Survey* 1978, p. 198.

Young girl who sells food outside a workers' hostel.

Photo: Rick Kollektiff

Black workers in "whites only" restaurant.

Photo: Tony McGrath

Street hawkers selling
offal.
Photo: Rick Kollektiff

4. SOCIAL SERVICES

"Disease and illness do not strike at random in South Africa, but along very definite channels of class and colour . . . It is not the inadequate penetration of a medical technology that produces these disease statistics, but the inadequate socio-political environment in which the black population is encapsulated. In sum . . . food, housing, employment opportunities and other similar non-medical factors play the decisive role in determining the morbidity and mortality rates."
— Professor M. Savage, addressing the South African Labour and Development Unit (Saldru) of the University of Cape Town in 1978.[1]

In a rural area.   Photo: Tony McGrath

Farm workers complain
about diet.
Photo: Camera Press

Social services such as health care, pensions, and welfare payments could not remedy the destructive effects of apartheid on the black people of South Africa. However, an adequate system of care would at least serve to shield the community against the worst horrors of disease and deprivation.

African women, with their double disability of sex and race, their disadvantages in employment possibilities, their lack of elementary rights even when compared with African men, and their vulnerability caused by their unique problems and daunting responsibilities in caring for their children, are particularly in need of social services.

Insofar as such services exist for Africans, however, they can not be called adequate.

In the field of health, the government's main achievement has been the building of a select number of showpiece hospitals like Baragwanath in Johannesburg. Apologists have described the South African Department of Health's policy as "a comprehensive approach aimed at total patient care in a system, which, although hospital-based, is essentially community orientated."[2]

The facts show these to be empty words. For instance:

★ In 1976-8 tuberculosis continued to occur in epidemic proportions amongst Africans—the incidence was more than 50 times that occurring among whites.[3]

★ Nearly 50% of African and Indian children admitted to the King Edward VIII Hospital in Durban betweeen 1970 and 1975 were seriously malnourished, to the extent that a quarter of them died.[4] The situation was worse in the bantustans: 75-80% of children admitted to two hospitals in the Transkei in 1972 were malnourished.[5]

★ Africans, particularly in the rural areas, suffer from diseases of malnutrition like kwashiorkor, pellagra, marasmus and beri-beri.[6]

★ In 1978 infant mortality among blacks was five times that of whites.[7]

A survey carried out in 1978 in the Msinga district of KwaZulu bantustan by the Church of Scotland Hospital concluded that it was impossible to accept that the government's policy of "comprehensive health care" was a serious one when no money was made available for essential services.[8]

On a wattle farm in Natal
owned by a British company.
Photo: Camera Press

A crippled woman in
Soweto.
Photo: Rick Kollektiff

In the field of care for the aged, in 1978 there were a total of four old age homes for Africans in the entire country—not one in Soweto, with a population of over a million people.[9]

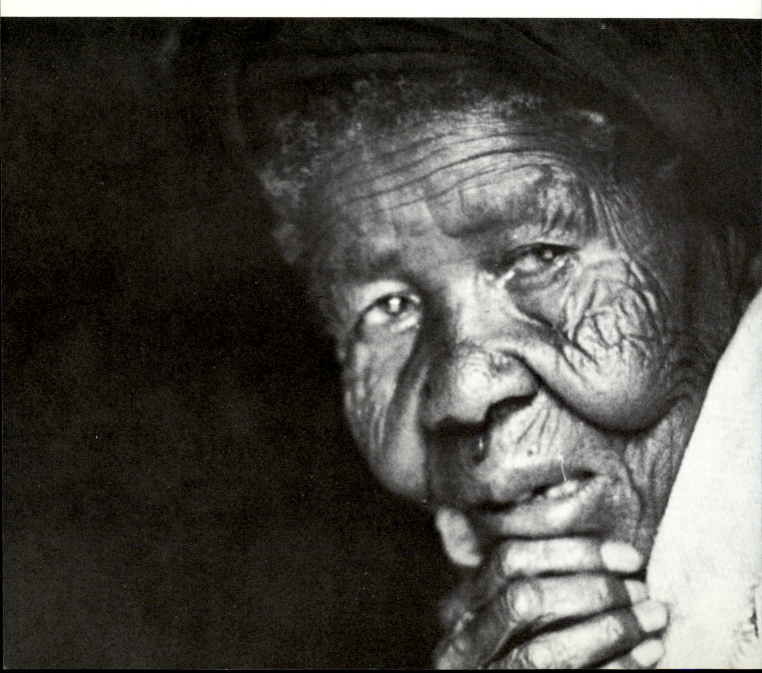

Old woman mending
her skirt.
Photo: Ralph Ndawo

(opposite)
Crippled old woman.
Photo: Tony McGrath

Beggar on Johannesburg
pavement.
Photo: Gerhard Cohn

(opposite)
Homeless woman.
Photo: Rick Kollektiff

Old woman foraging
in rubbish bins.
Photographer Unknown

The story is the same when it comes to recreational facilities. South Africa is justly world famous for the outdoor sports opportunities it provides for its white population, women as well as men. Black women, however, must make the best of whatever resources are at hand.

Bowls tournament in Port Elizabeth.

Photo: Tony McGrath

White sunbathers. Note
black cleaner.
Photo: Tony McGrath

A waterhole in a rural area.

Photo: Tony McGrath

Traditional dancing.   Photo: Tony McGrath

The grotesque inadequacy of the social services for black people was illustrated in November 1978 by a report in the Johannesburg *Post* that the International Committee of the Red Cross were investigating the possibility of rendering assistance to needy children—not in devastated Kampuchea or Bangladesh, but in one of the richest countries of the world: South Africa.[10]

Restaurant for whites only in Hillbrow, Johannesburg.   Photo: Tony McGrath

Eating lunch on side-walk, Johannesburg.   Photo: Stan Winer

1 South African Institute of Race Relations *Survey* 1978, p. 467.
2 Ibid., p. 466, quoting from *The Health of the People*, C. J. van Rensburg Publications 1977.
3 Ibid., p. 467.
4 Ibid., p. 468.
5 Barbara Rogers, *Divide and Rule* (IDAF, London, 1976) p. 30.
6 South African Institute of Race Relations *Survey* 1978, pp. 467-8.
7 South African Institute of Race Relations *Survey* 1978, p. 467.
8 Ibid., p. 466.
9 Ibid., p. 484.
10 Ibid., p. 484.

Crossroads, Cape Town.   Photo: Eckhard Supp

5. SQUATTER CAMPS
A revolt against the migrant labour system

"The women of Crossroads called a meeting, and in this way committees were formed. Only the women. With this delegation we went to speak to the authorities. Why are you so hard on us? we asked. We are doing no harm. The Police Commissioner who heard us didn't even bother to reply. He only showed us the paper that says Crossroads must go."
— A woman of Crossroads, interviewed on Dutch television, 1978.[1]

Crossroads, Cape Town.
Photo: Eckhard Supp

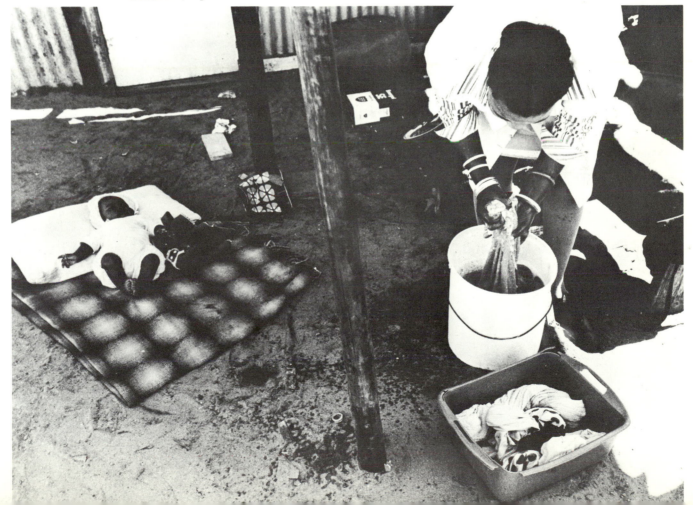

Building a shack.   Photo: Steve Bloom

One of the most notable developments arising out of ordinary people's courage and ingenuity in resisting apartheid has been the squatter camps. The position of women and family life were central to this development, and women and their organisations such as the Crossroads Women's Movement played a major role in organising and defending the camps.

Squatter camps are a grassroots revolt against the migrant labour system. They have been set up in various parts of the country, but particularly in the Cape Peninsula because it is in this region that the effects of the system have been most acute. The government declared the Cape Peninsula a "preferential labour area" for Coloured (mixed race) people, the eventual aim being to rid the Peninsula of Africans as far as possible.

Winterveld, outside Pretoria.   Photo: Rick Kollektiff

A well in Winterveld.
Photo: Rick Kollektiff

Influx control was then enforced with particur harshness, and the building of houses suitable for family accommodation was stopped in the three main African townships: in Langa in 1955, in Nyanga in 1962, in Guguletu in 1972. Africans were thenceforward supposed to enter the area on a yearly basis only, to spend 11 months at a time in the "bachelor hostels."

Many Africans, however, were long-term residents of Cape Town. In Crossroads camp the average time of residence in the city was 18.2 years for the men and 11.7 years for the women.[2]

Searching for food in municipal rubbish tips, South of Johannesburg. Photo: Rick Kollektiff

These people rejected the system. In 1975 they begun setting up their own shanty towns, with a tremendous community spirit. Crossroads, for instance, with no policing apart from what the residents themselves could provide, had an incidence of crime far lower than the government-administered "Bantu townships".[3] Health statistics compared favourably with those in the rest of the Peninsula and were better than those in the bantustans.[4] The residents organised their own amenities: schools, community centres, churches.

In 1977 and 1978 the squatters' camps of Werkgenot, Modderdam and Unibell were demolished and most of the residents deported to the bantustans. Of the 10,000 residents of Unibell, for instance, only 46 were rehoused locally, after a demolition carried out "with total disregard for the health and well-being of the residents."[5]

Woman bitten by police dog during demolition of Modderdam.   Photographer Unknown

(opposite)
Searching for food in
municipal rubbish tips,
South of Johannesburg.
Photo: Rick Kollektiff

In Modderdam, shortly after its demolition.
Photographer Unknown

Demolition of Unibel, Cape Town.

Photo: Peter Magubane

The brutality of the demolitions, and the spirit and resourcefulness of the squatters, caught the attention of the world. An international campaign was mobilised to save the remaining camp, Crossroads, which was subjected to continual police raids in June and September 1978. The women of Crossroads, through the Crossroads Women's Committee, played a major part in the resistance.

The campaign was defused in November 1978 when the Minister of Plural Relations and Development, Dr. P. Koornhof, announced that the scheduled demolition of Crossroads would not take place. Dr. Koornhof stated that most squatters would be rehoused locally.[6] It was announced in February 1981 that about 20,000 Crossroads residents would be granted permanent resident status in the Western Cape.[7] (Estimates of the original population of Crossroads varied between 23,000 and 40,000).

However, *The Guardian* of 4 October 1979 reported the Deputy Minister, Dr. G. de V. Morrison, as stating that only "a quarter" of the Crossroads residents would be rehoused locally; the other 18,000 people who constituted 3,600 families were "totally and unacceptably illegally" in the Cape and would be removed to the bantustans.

[1] *Apartheid Inside Outside,* Roeland Kerbosch Film Produksie, Amsterdam, 1978.
[2] South African Institute of Race Relations, *Survey* 1978, p. 352.
[3] Ibid., p. 353.
[4] Ibid., p. 353.
[5] Ibid., p. 352.
[6] *The Guardian,* 10 December 1978.
[7] *Cape Times,* 28 February 1981.

Police with dogs raid Crossroads, 14 September 1978.   Photographer Unknown

Her husband was arrested
in police raid on Crossroads,
14 September 1978.
Photo: Eckhard Supp

6.   WOMEN AGAINST APARTHEID:
Mass Campaigns 1913-59

"Now you have touched the women you have struck a rock
You have dislodged a boulder
You will be crushed."
— Women's Anti-Pass Campaign Song, 1956.

Lilian Ngoyi, President of Women's Federation
at pass protest, Zeerust, Western Transvaal, 1957.

Photographer Unknown

Women have always taken part with men in the battle against apartheid; but in addition to the campaigns and activities involving both sexes in the struggle to achieve national liberation, women have campaigned additionally on issues primarily affecting them as women.

Meeting of Federation of South African Women, Johannesburg 1954.   Photo: Eli Weinberg

Recruiting for Campaign of Defiance of Unjust Laws, 1952.
Photo: Jurgen Schadeburg

Natal Indian women's delegation to the Congress of the People, 1955.   Photo: Eli Weinberg

In 1913 in the Orange Free State, African women living in urban townships were made to buy a new entry permit each month. The women organised petitions and deputations against the permits, and, when these failed, mass marches in Bloemfontein and Winberg. The struggle ended in victory for the women: the permits were withdrawn.

In 1955 the Minister of Native Affairs announced that African women would be issued with passes from January 1956. Up to then, only men had had to carry passes.

90

An arrest under the pass laws.
Photo: Eli Weinberg

WE
STAND
BY OUR
WE
STAND
BY OUR
LEADERS
WE
STAND
BY OUR
LEADERS

Protesting against passes for
women, Union Buildings,
Pretoria, 1956.
Photo: Rand Daily Mail

(previous page)
Demonstration outside
Treason Trial Court,
Johannesburg, 1956.
Photo: Eli Weinberg

The first big protest against passes for women took place in October 1955 with 2,000 women, mainly Africans, converging on Pretoria.

The women's anti-pass movement grew. Marches and demonstrations took place nationwide. On 9 August 1956, 20,000 women from all over the country assembled in Pretoria to protest. This day has since been designated "Women's Day" in South Africa.

The women's leaders delivered a petition to the Prime Minister's office.

In line with government policy at the time, which was to ignore all representations from Africans, the Prime Minister was not available to see the delegation.

Demonstration against passes for women, Johannesburg City Hall, 1957.　　　Photo: Rand Daily Mail

Demonstration against passes, Johannesburg City Hall, 1957.   Photographer Unknown

The issue of passes proceeded, but so did the protests, which spread even into the remote countryside—notably into the Zeerust area of the Transvaal where in one village only 76 out of 4,000 women accepted the passes. A terrible punishment was visited on them by the police. People were shot, beaten, and their homes were burned to the ground.

At the same time, women were protesting about the beerhall system. The law prevented Africans from brewing traditional beer; however men were allowed to patronise municipal beerhalls. The women argued that they should be allowed to brew, in accordance with customs of traditional hospitality, and that the halls should be closed.

Peasant women protest against the issuing of pass books to women, Zeerust, Western Transvaal, 1957.
Photographer Unknown

In June 1959 2,000 women gathered at Cator Manor, Durban, to express their grievances about beerhalls. The police charged the women with batons, striking them down with the utmost brutality, often hitting the babies strapped to their backs.

Women protest at Cato Manor, Durban, 1959.

Photographer Unknown

Police attack women demonstrators at Cato Manor, Durban, 1959.   Photo: Laurie Bloomfield

Again, the protests spread. There were more baton charges, and mass arrests.

The spirit of the women remained undimmed but events made peaceful mass action impossible after 1959.

The struggle had taken a new turning.

*This account is taken from that given by Hilda Bernstein in her book *For their Triumphs and for their Tears* (IDAF, London, 1978) pp. 45-9.

Keep My Baby
Alive!
Pay Me R2 a Day
Recognise
My Trade Union
Support SACTU's
SACTU
Demands:
• Living Wages
• R2.00 a Day
• The Right To Organ
• The Right To Bargain
With Our Bosses
• Decent Treatment
• Shorter Hours
We Must Eat More Than
Mielie

7. WOMEN AGAINST APARTHEID:
The Struggle Continues 1960 –

"Colour bars retard the process of female emancipation by impeding the progress of the whole race. Women therefore choose to fight along with their men for full civic rights rather than against the men for legal and social equality. By taking part in the national movement against racial discrimination, women have established a claim to equality. This can become a reality, however, only when both women and men have become full citizens in a free society."
— H. J. Simons, *African Women: their Legal Status in South Africa.*[1]

Demonstration on 4th anniversary of Treason Trial, December 1960.   Photographer Unknown

(opposite)
Demonstration by two militants
of the South African Congress
of Trade Unions.
Photographer Unknown

Mrs. Luthuli mourns
at Chief A. J. Luthuli's
funeral, July 1967.
Photo: Peter Magubane

The Sharpeville shootings of March 1960; the State of Emergency that followed; the banning of the ANC and PAC; and the great purge of political activists after the enactment of the "Sabotage Act" and the no-trial detention laws of the early 1960s, changed the pattern of the women's struggle.

Their organisations were destroyed. If they weren't banned outright, like the ANC Women's League, they were rendered inoperative by the individual banning of members. The non-racial Federation of South African Women had nearly all its leading members banned, including its President, Lilian Ngoyi; the Federation's Secretary, Helen Joseph, was the first person to be placed under house arrest.

Police baton charge demonstration, Johannesburg, 1972.   Photographer Unknown

(opposite) Arrest of demonstrator outside Supreme Court, Johannesburg, March 1975.   Photo: Alf Kuma

Mrs. Dhana Naidu protests at her eviction from her Pageview, Johannesburg home after the area was declared white.

Photo: Peter Magubane

No political organisation representing black women has since been able to exist for long. In 1975 the Black Women's Federation was established with the object of linking black groups to practical activities, such as schemes to inform women of their rights, and to reduce the cost of school uniforms. Even these activities were unacceptable to the government. The Black Women's Federation was banned in 1977 along with other organisations.

But bans have not succeeded in crushing resistance. New organisations continually emerge to replace the banned ones. After the banning of the Black Women's Federation in 1977, there emerged the Women's Federation of South Africa. It played a major part in the campaigns of 1980 and 1981, against rent increases, against compulsory education and against the celebrations of the twentieth anniversary of the apartheid republic.

Women have continued to organise among themselves in every field. On many occasions women workers have taken strike action over the very low wages they are generally paid.

Rita Ndzanga, a trade unionist, at the graveside of her husband Lawrence who died in police detention.
Photographer Unknown

Young woman wounded
by police bullet during
demonstration in Soweto.
Photo: Peter Magubane

(opposite)
Woman injured in police
attack on striking workers,
Johannesburg, March 1976.
Photographer Unknown

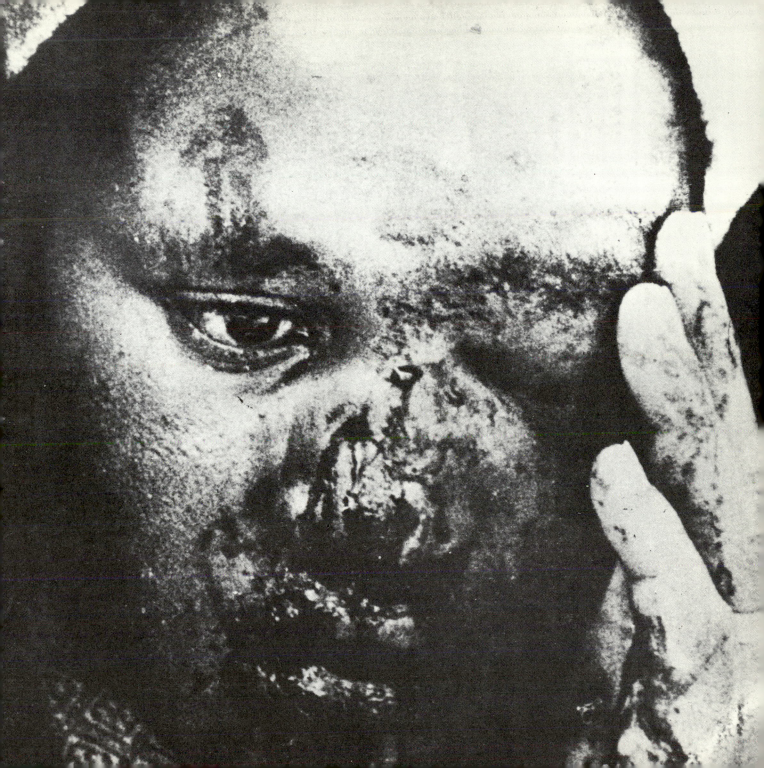

Martha Mahlangu, mother of Solomon Mahlangu, ANC guerilla, executed by South African regime.
Photographer Unknown

Ntsikie Biko, wife of Steve Biko, interviewed by overseas press after leaving court of enquiry into her husband's death.
Photographer Unknown

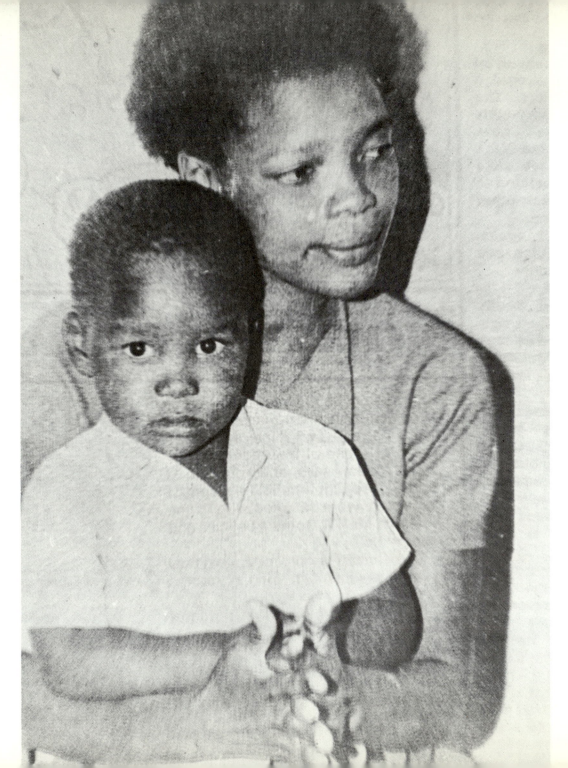

Wife and child of James Mange, ANC guerilla, sentenced to death (later commuted to 20 years' imprisonment) by South African regime. Photographer Unknown

Winnie Mandela, wife of Nelson Mandela, speaking at Black Women's Federation meeting.

Photo: Peter Magubane

Women and men organise and fight together against apartheid. Together they have been banned, detained, imprisoned, tortured, and killed. Some have been forced into exile, and continue outside the country to fight against apartheid. Others, like Thandi Modise, left South Africa after the uprising of 1976 to obtain military training, and returned as guerillas. Thandi Modise is now in prison along with other women who have contributed to the armed struggle for liberation by recruiting people for military training or assisting guerillas.

Demonstrator.
Photo: Alf Kumalo

(previous page)
Demonstration outside
court in support of
"Pretoria 12", 21 June 1977.
Photographer Unknown

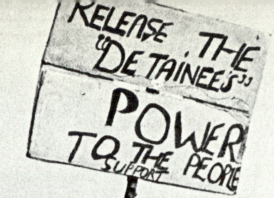

Young woman demanding release
of Soweto student leaders.

Photo: Gamma

Winnie Mandela, who has played a leading part in women's organisations, campaigns and activities since her membership of the ANC Women's League, has become an international symbol of resistance. She has suffered endless persecution. For more than a decade she has been banned, arrested and re-arrested, tried and re-tried, detained and re-detained, held in solitary confinement for months at a time, and banished to a remote and hostile area where she is subjected to continual scrutiny and harrassment by the police.

Hilda Bernstein writes:

". . . victory in the struggle against apartheid is the absolute condition for any change in the social status of women as a whole."[2]

---

*This account is taken from that given by Hilda Bernstein in her *For their Triumphs and for their Tears* (IDAF, London, 1978) pp. 50-66.

[1] Hurst, London, 1968.
[2] *For their Triumphs and for their Tears*, pp. 61-2.

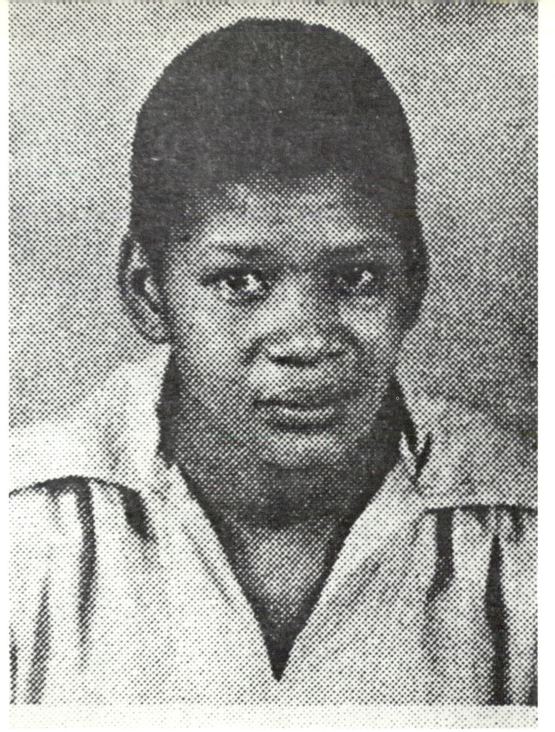

Thandi Modise, ANC guerilla, now serving an eight year prison sentence. She is the first woman in South
Africa to be convicted, under the Terrorism Act, for undergoing military training.   Photographer Unknown

Printed in England by A G Bishop & Sons Ltd, Orpington, Kent.